More praise for STITCHES

"Throughout, Small's art—by turns expressively abstract and clinically realistic—ensures that *Stitches* lands on the reader with satisfying emotional weight . . . palpably, recognizably human."

—Glen Weldon, NPR.org

"[Small] shows, in ways that dozens of traditional memoirs rarely accomplish with thousands of words, a distinct brand of stony Midwestern stoicism, and watchfulness, and with few panels, captures the small moments when chilliness veers into empathy, and vice versa."

—Christopher Borrelli, *Chicago Tribune*

"The honesty, seamlessness and extraordinary play of light make David Small's *Stitches* singularly cutting and moving."

—Carlo Wolff, *Boston Sunday Globe*

"Small has made a truly beautiful story and book."

—Ken Tucker, *Entertainment Weekly*

"His expressive, impressionistic brushstrokes and ink-wash shading are well suited to the subtleties of observat⋯

⋯as Wolk, *Bookforum*

"Like other 'importa⋯ ⋯iently disturbing, pitch-black funny,⋯ ⋯hipman, *Booklist*

"[An] emotionally⋯ ⋯graphic memoir of childhood traum⋯ ⋯*Kirkus Reviews*

"He makes you be⋯

⋯onfiction of 2009

"Finally with *Stitch*⋯ ⋯s been bridged."

⋯a *Literary Review*

"This book stretches the envelope of what a graphic novel can achieve."

—Sol M. Davidson, *International Journal of Comic Art*

"The melding of memoir and graphic novel is one of those alchemical developments which we can point to, gratefully, as a recent beacon of hope for the printed word. Paging through *Stitches*, a reader is certain that there is no other way that Small's story might have been told."

—Spike Jonze Blog

"*Stitches* has the rare distinction of being both whimsical and horrific, and yet there is an innocence that makes the book so genuine and heartbreaking, I was unable to stop reading until I was out of pages."

—Lindsay Champion, BiblioBuffet.com

"Pain shared lightens the load of the sufferer. Pain transformed lifts the load of all of us. By that standard, *Stitches* is not just the most unusual book you'll ever read—it's a public service."

—Jesse Kornbluth, *Huffington Post*

"In his graphic memoir, *Stitches*, Small telegraphs the gothic horror of his childhood with remarkably disturbing, impressionistic, often poetic illustrations."

—Becky Ohlsen, Bookmunch.com

"*Stitches* is the product of a child's pain and an adult's understanding of the world; Small is clear-eyed and sympathetic, intuitive and angry, and his images are so innate, so of a piece with his carefully parsed words, that they seem to seep off the page and into the reader's head."

—Molly Templeton, *Eugene Weekly*

"Like the boy in this autobiographical novel, my first reading of *Stitches* left me speechless. And in awe. David Small presents us with a profound and moving gift of graphic literature that has the look of a movie and reads like a poem. Spare in words, painful in pictures, Small, in a style of dry menace, draws us a boy's life that you wouldn't want to live but you can't put down. From its first line four pages in, 'Mama had her little cough,' we know that we are in the hands of a master."

—Jules Feiffer, Pulitzer Prize–winning cartoonist

"David Small's *Stitches* is aptly named. With surgical precision, the author pierces into the past and, with great artistry, seals the wound inflicted on a small child by cruel and unloving parents. *Stitches* is as intensely dramatic as a woodcut novel of the silent movie era and as fluid as a contemporary Japanese manga. It breaks new ground for graphic novels."

—Françoise Mouly, art editor, *The New Yorker*; editorial director, TOON Books

"David Small evokes the mad scientific world of the 1950s beautifully, a time when everyone believed that science could fix everything. Small is an innocent lamb, a sensitive boy, caught in a nightmare situation. His parents and grandmother are really creepy. Capturing body language and facial expressions subtly, *Stitches* becomes in Small's skillful hands a powerful story, an emotionally charged autobiography." —R. Crumb, author of *The Book of Genesis*

"Add David Small's book to the illustrated bible of artists who have had to will themselves— invent themselves—and ultimately seize success as the only way to keep the gritty, dark beginning of a home life from snuffing them out altogether. If this book were a wine you'd discover a nose full of Truffot, Baudelaire and John Waters. And yet, after all the blows, and the despair, and the desperation, David Small skillfully manages to draw a door out of his past and invite us into his present."

—Jack Gantos, author of *Joey Pigza Swallowed the Key*, finalist for the National Book Award

"In *Stitches*, David Small exposes the deepest part of a painful youth—cathartic and disturbing as memoirs get by one of our most gifted storytellers. This one will resonate long after you put it down." —Harry Bliss, cover artist for *The New Yorker* and illustrator of three *New York Times* bestsellers: *A Fine, Fine School*; *Diary of a Worm, Diary of a Spider*; and *Diary of a Fly*

"*Stitches* is one of the most compelling books I've read in a long time—totally original in style, seemingly simplistic while psychologically complex and totally absorbing. There's no doubt that David Small, with his groundbreaking work, has elevated the art of the graphic novel and brought it to new creative heights." —Stan Lee, co-creator of *Spider-Man*

"An unforgettable picture of a harrowing childhood."

—Scott McCloud, author of *Understanding Comics*

"I'm not being hyperbolic when I say that I think it stands up with *Contract With God* or *Maus* in the canon of graphic novels." —Michael Schumacher, biographer of Will Eisner

STITCHES

a memoir...

DAVID SMALL

W. W. Norton & Company
New York · London

To Mark Stewart Guin and to my brother, Ted

For information about permission to reproduce selections from this book,
write to Permissions, W. W. Norton & Company, Inc.,
500 Fifth Avenue, New York, NY 10110

For information about special discounts for bulk purchases, please contact
W. W. Norton Special Sales at specialsales@wwnorton.com or 800-233-4830

Manufacturing by Courier Westford
Book design by Paul Buckley
Production manager: Anna Oler

Library of Congress Cataloging-in-Publication Data

Small, David, 1945-
Stitches : a memoir— / David Small.
p. cm.
ISBN 978-0-393-06857-3 (hardcover)
1. Small, David, 1945—Comic books, strips, etc. 2. Authors, American—20th century—Biography—Comic books, strips, etc.
3. Artists—United States—Biography—Comic books, strips, etc. 4. Children's stories—Illustrations—
Comic books, strips, etc. 5. Children's stories—Authorship—Comic books, strips, etc. I. Title.
PN6727.S54465S75 2009
818'.5409—dc22
[B]
                                                                            2009022526

ISBN 978-0-393-33896-6 pbk.

W. W. Norton & Company, Inc.
500 Fifth Avenue, New York, N.Y. 10110
www.wwnorton.com

W. W. Norton & Company Ltd.
Castle House, 75/76 Wells Street, London W1T 3QT

2 3 4 5 6 7 8 9 0

STITCHES

DETROIT

13

MAMA HAD HER LITTLE COUGH . . .

ONCE OR TWICE, SOME QUIET SOBBING, OUT OF SIGHT . . .

OR THE SLAMMING OF KITCHEN CUPBOARD DOORS.

THAT WAS HER LANGUAGE.

THE MERE MOVING OF HER FORK A HALF-INCH TO THE RIGHT SPELLED DREAD AT THE DINNER TABLE.

HER FURIOUS, SILENT WITHDRAWALS COULD LAST FOR DAYS, EVEN WEEKS AT A TIME.

BECAUSE SHE NEVER SPOKE HER MIND, WE NEVER KNEW WHAT THIS WAS ALL ABOUT.

WE TWO BOYS DIDN'T, AT ANY RATE.

DAD, HOME FROM WORK, WENT DOWN TO THE BASEMENT AND
THUMPED A PUNCHING BAG. THAT WAS HIS LANGUAGE.

MY BROTHER, TED,
BEAT ON HIS DRUM.

AND I, TOO, HAD LEARNED
A WAY OF EXPRESSING MYSELF
WORDLESSLY . . .

GETTING SICK, THAT WAS MY LANGUAGE.

I WAS BORN ANXIOUS AND ANGRY. MY SINUSES AND DIGESTIVE SYSTEM DIDN'T WORK AS THEY SHOULD HAVE.

HOWEVER, DAD WAS A DOCTOR.

HE KNEW WHAT TO DO.

DAD PRESCRIBED THE MEDICINES FOR MY FREQUENT BOUTS WITH THIS AND THAT.

DAD GAVE ME SHOTS

AND ENEMAS.

DAD PUT ME ON HIS TREATMENT TABLE AND "CRACKED MY NECK," OUR FAMILY NICKNAME FOR THE OSTEOPATHIC MANIPULATIONS HE HAD LEARNED IN MEDICAL SCHOOL.

AND IT WAS DAD THE RADIOLOGIST WHO GAVE ME THE MANY X-RAYS THAT WERE SUPPOSED TO CURE MY SINUS PROBLEMS.

WEEKNIGHTS WE DROVE TO PICK UP DAD FROM WORK.
PUBLIC PARKING WAS IN THE REAR OF THE HOSPITAL, BUT MAMA ALWAYS DROVE DOWN THE RAMP TO THE DELIVERY ENTRANCE AND PARKED THERE.

AS THE FORD'S TIRES SCREECHED DOWN THE STEEP SLOPE . . .

MY BROTHER AND I WENT INTO ECSTATIC SCREAMING FITS AS WE IMAGINED . . .

OUR MOTHER TAKING HER FOOT OFF THE BRAKE . . .

THE CAR HURTLING DOWN THE SLOPE . . .

AND SMASHING TO BITS.

WE ENTERED THE HOSPITAL THROUGH THE BASEMENT, PASSING THE CAFETERIA, THE PHARMACY AND THE LAUNDRY, ALL CLOSED FOR THE NIGHT.

EACH TIME IT SMELLED THE SAME: CARBOLIC ACID, MEATLOAF OR CHICKEN, AND BLEACH.

IN A WARREN OF SMALL OFFICES AND IN A CLOUD OF SMOKE WE FOUND DAD . . .

. . . PORING OVER X-RAYS WITH THE OTHER RADIOLOGISTS.

TO ME, DAD AND HIS COLLEAGUES SEEMED LIKE THE HEROIC MEN FEATURED IN THE ADS IN **LIFE** MAGAZINE, MARCHING BRAVELY INTO THE BRIGHT AND SHINING FUTURE.

THEY WERE SOLDIERS OF SCIENCE, AND THEIR WEAPON WAS THE X-RAY. X-RAYS COULD SEE THROUGH CLOTHES, SKIN, EVEN METAL. THEY WERE MIRACULOUS WONDER RAYS THAT WOULD CURE ANYTHING.

MY BROTHER AND I LIKED SEEING THE X-RAYS OF LITTLE KIDS' STOMACHS, THE STUFF THEY HAD SWALLOWED LIKE KEYS AND POP BEADS . . .

. . . AND CRACKER-JACK PRIZES.

I'LL BE A WHILE, BETTY, BOYS . . .

TAKE A SEAT IN MY OFFICE.

DING!

I HAD NEVER BEEN ON THE FOURTH FLOOR. HERE, EVERYONE HAD GONE HOME FOR THE NIGHT. THE AIR SMELLED OF FRESH FLOOR WAX.

AND THERE BEFORE ME, WITH ITS NEWLY POLISHED LINOLEUM . . .

. . . WAS THE PERFECT SOCK-SKATING RINK.

SENT TO BED WITH
NO SUPPER, I DREAMED
THAT NIGHT OF THE
LITTLE MAN IN THE JAR.

THE NEXT DAY, EVEN AFTER THE HOSPITAL CALLED TO SAY THAT MY SHOES HAD BEEN FOUND . . .

THANK YOU.

MAMA STAYED ANGRY.

WHAP!

HER SILENT FURY WAS LIKE A BLACK TIDAL WAVE. EITHER YOU GET OUT OF THE WAY, OR . . .

I HAD FALLEN IN LOVE
WITH ALICE.

ESPECIALLY WITH

HER LONG

BLONDE

HAIR.

I THOUGHT IT MUST BE HER HAIR
THAT GAVE ALICE THE MAGIC ABILITY
TO TRAVEL TO A LAND OF
TALKING ANIMALS, SINGING FLOWERS
AND DANCING TEAPOTS.

I WANTED TO GO THERE IMMEDIATELY.

FAG!
QUEER! HOMO!
SISSY!

DURING SPRING VACATION OUR FAMILY SPLIT DOWN THE MIDDLE. DAD TOOK TED AND HEADED EAST TO VISIT HIS OLD MOTHER, WHILE MAMA TOOK ME AND DROVE SOUTH TO BE WITH HERS.

IT WAS A LONG TRIP BETWEEN DETROIT AND SOUTHEASTERN
INDIANA ON TWO-LANE ROADS ALL THE WAY.

THERE WAS NO RADIO IN THE CAR, AND NO AIR-CONDITIONING.

WITH THE WINDOWS UP, THE CAR WAS A FURNACE.

WINDOWS DOWN, IT WAS A WIND TUNNEL.

AS EVENING CAME ON, THE AIR BEGAN TO COOL, THE LAND BEGAN TO ROLL, AND MAMA—USUALLY SO STERNLY SILENT—BEGAN TO TALK. SHE TOLD ME HER FAMILY STORIES.

MY GRANDPARENTS (MAMA'S MAMA AND PAPA) HAD MET AT A DANCE.

BOTH OF THEM LIKED A GOOD TIME, SO THEY KEPT ON MEETING AND KEPT ON DANCING, UNTIL, SUDDENLY . . .

THEY NEEDED TO GET MARRIED.

BUT HIS PARENTS (MY GREAT-GRANDPARENTS, THE MURPHYS) DIDN'T APPROVE OF DANCING AND THEY DIDN'T APPROVE OF HER.

White Trash Tramp!

SO THEY ELOPED.

NOW MAN AND WIFE, THEY MOVED INTO A ONE-ROOM CABIN ON THE BACK OF THE MURPHY PROPERTY. BECAUSE THE MURPHYS WOULD NOT ALLOW HER TO HAVE HER BABY IN THEIR HOUSE, MAMA WAS BORN IN THAT CABIN.

THE DOCTOR COULD NOT FIND HER HEARTBEAT. HE BELIEVED SHE WAS DEAD, YET SOMEHOW STILL BREATHING.

THEN HE DISCOVERED HER HEART. IT WAS OVER ON THE WRONG SIDE OF HER CHEST.

MAMA'S FATHER DIED WHEN SHE WAS TEN. HE AND TWO FRIENDS HAD BEEN OUT DRINKING AND, WHILE DRIVING HOME IN THE DARK, SAILED OVER A CLIFF.

AFTER THE FUNERAL GREAT-GRANDMOTHER MURPHY BECAME MORE CRUEL TOWARDS HER DAUGHTER-IN-LAW.

SHE CUT OFF THE MONEY AND FORCED HER OFF THE PROPERTY.

GRANDMA AND MAMA MOVED TO CONNERSVILLE WHERE, FOR A TIME, GRANDMA CLEANED HOUSES. THEN SHE REMARRIED.

GREAT-GRANDFATHER MURPHY TRIED TO KILL HIMSELF BY DRINKING DRANO.

ALTHOUGH HE LIVED, HE NEVER SPOKE ANOTHER WORD. THE POISON HAD EATEN AWAY HIS VOCAL CORDS.

FINALLY, WHEN GREAT-GRANDMOTHER
MURPHY DIED, EVERYONE LEARNED
SHE HAD BEEN A PETTY THIEF.
HER BEDROOM CHEST WAS STUFFED
WITH PIECEGOODS: LADIES' KID
GLOVES, RIBBONS, LENGTHS OF
SILK AND SPOOLS OF LACE.

IN ALL HER YEARS OF STEALING
SHE HAD NEVER BEEN STOPPED.

AFTER EACH VISIT TO
THE DRY-GOODS STORE
THE OWNER WOULD CALL
MR. MURPHY, WHO
PROMPTLY (AND OF COURSE,
QUIETLY) CAME DOWN
AND PAID THE BILL.

GRANDMA'S HOUSE LOOKED TO ME LIKE THE GINGERBREAD HOUSE FROM "HANSEL AND GRETL."

MY STEP-GRANDFATHER, PAPA JOHN, CAME HOME FROM WORK.

PAPA JOHN HAD A SCRATCHY FACE. HE WORE A WATCH AND CHAIN.

HE WAS THE "GREETER" AT A FUNERAL HOME.

HE TOOK ME TO SEE THE TRAINS COME IN.

PAPA JOHN KNEW EVERYONE IN TOWN.

HE KNEW ALL THE "BOYS" AT THE BAR.

PAPA JOHN HAD HIS OWN TEETH. GRANDMA DIDN'T.

AFTER SUPPER, THE GROWNUPS SAT IN THE YARD TALKING . . .

WHILE I CAUGHT FIREFLIES AND PUT THEM IN A JAR.

MAMA TOOK ME UP TO BED. GRANDMA'S BATHROOM WAS PINK AND FULL OF A GASSY SMELL.

I SOON FELL ASLEEP.

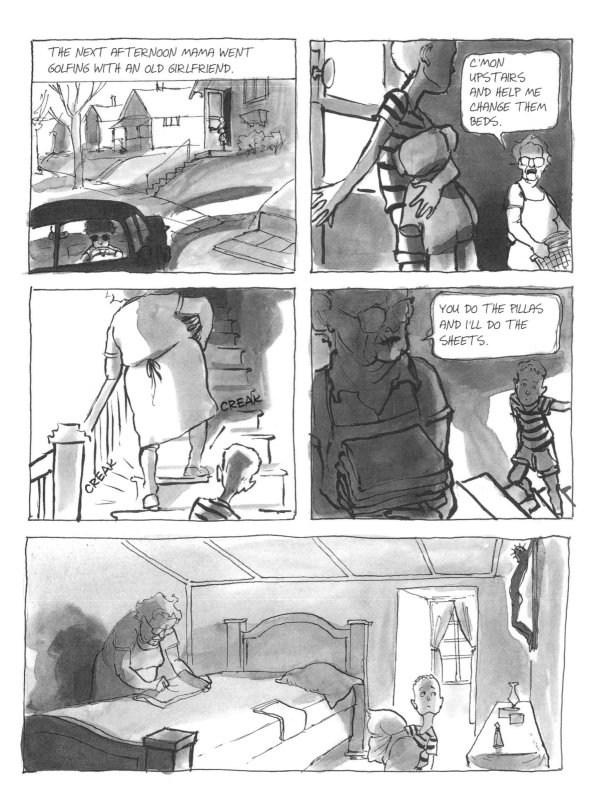

THE NEXT AFTERNOON MAMA WENT GOLFING WITH AN OLD GIRLFRIEND.

C'MON UPSTAIRS AND HELP ME CHANGE THEM BEDS.

CREAK

CREAK

YOU DO THE PILLAS AND I'LL DO THE SHEETS.

QUIT DAWDLIN' AND GIT THEM CASES ON!

WHY...

YOU DURN LITTLE FOOL!

YOU'VE GOT TO LEARN!

GRANDMA!
MAY I
GO DOWN
AND PLAY?

YES.
GO ON
WITH YOU!

THE REST OF THE DAY I PLAYED QUIETLY BY MYSELF

AND STEERED CLEAR
OF GRANDMA.

THIS MAY SOUND ODD, BUT WHILE THAT WAS HAPPENING . . .

I SAW IT ALL FROM TWO POINTS-OF-VIEW, HERS AND MINE.

ON THE ONE HAND, I FELT THE FEAR, HUMILIATION AND PAIN . . .

WHILE ON THE OTHER, FOR REASONS I COULD NOT QUITE UNDERSTAND . . .

I FELT THAT SHE WAS JUSTIFIED . . .

AND THAT I DESERVED EVERYTHING I HAD GOTTEN.

99

NOW BOTH OF THEM WERE ANGRY WITH ME.
THE LITTLE ROOM FELT AS CLOSE AS A COFFIN.

HE WAS A **DURN** LITTLE FOOL!

I WAS ELEVEN

DETROIT

WHEN THE HOSPITAL WOMEN'S AUXILIARY BRIDGE CLUB MET AT OUR HOUSE I ANSWERED THE DOOR AND CARRIED THE LADIES' COATS UPSTAIRS . . .

WHY, DAVID! HOW YOU'VE GROWN!

. . A JOB I LIKED BECAUSE IT INVOLVED CARRYING MRS. DILLON'S MINK.

I HAD A MAD CRUSH ON MRS. DILLON.

THE WIFE OF A SURGEON, SHE HAD FOR ME AN ALMOST SUPERNATURAL GLAMOUR AND SOPHISTICATION.

SHE DRANK MANHATTANS.

SHE LIKED THE MUSIC OF DAVE BRUBECK.

KLIK!

SHE WAS VERSED IN THE FILMS OF BRIGITTE BARDOT . . .

. . . BUT THEN WHO'S WATCHING HER ACTING?

HA! HA! HA!

AND SHE LEFT THE SCARLET IMPRINT OF HER LIPS ON THE REMAINS OF HER FILTER-TIPPED CIGARETTES.

ALSO ON THOSE ENCHANTED BRIDGE CLUB EVENINGS, SOMETHING HAPPENED TO MY MOTHER.

115

120

OF COURSE I'LL GET YOU TO A DOCTOR.

BUT, IN CASE YOU DON'T KNOW IT, LET ME TEACH YOU SOMETHING!

DOCTORS COST MONEY AND MONEY IS SOMETHING THAT IS IN SHORT SUPPLY IN THIS HOUSE!

132

AROUND THAT TIME DAD MUST HAVE GOTTEN A PROMOTION OR A RAISE. THE LUMP IN MY NECK HAD TO WAIT WHILE HE TOOK MOTHER ON A SHOPPING SPREE.

THIS WILL SURELY LEAD TO A COMPRESSION OF THE (PUFF) VERTEBRAE RESULTING IN PERMANENT DEFORMATION OF THE SPINE SUCH AS (PUFF PUFF) SCOLIOSIS OR SPONDYLOLISTHESIS. WE SEE THIS ALL THE TIME IN LATERAL CURVATURE (PUFF PUFF) AND ALSO IN THE EXAGGERATIONS OF THE ANTERO-POSTERIOR CURVES FOUND IN MOST CASES OF (PUFF PUFF) POOR POSTURE.

AS FOR YOUR STANDING POSITION, IF YOU GO ON WITH IT, YOUR LUMBAR WILL START TO FAIL TO UPHOLD YOUR DORSAL CURVE AND BOTH WILL BECOME EXAGGERATED.

THE RESULTANT LORDOSIS AND KYPHOSIS WILL GIVE YOU THAT FORWARD THRUST OF THE HEAD AND THE SUNKEN CHEST (PUFF PUFF PUFF); THAT LOOK OF CHRONIC FATIGUE WHICH WE SEE SO OFTEN IN OLD PEOPLE.

THREE AND A HALF
YEARS
AFTER THE FIRST
DIAGNOSIS

I WAS FOURTEEN

THAT NIGHT, BACK IN MY HOSPITAL ROOM, I WAS SURPRISED BY A VISIT FROM MY MOTHER.

WHAT ARE YOU DOING HERE?

173

STEP INSIDE YOUR MOUTH WITH ME FOR A MOMENT, WON'T YOU?

CAREFUL ON THE TONGUE! IT'S SLIPPERY!

NOW, YOU SEE DOWN THERE? THOSE FOLDING SCREENS OVER THE TUNNEL OF YOUR THROAT? THOSE ARE YOUR VOCAL CORDS. WHEN AIR FLOWS OVER THEM THEY VIBRATE LIKE THE STRINGS ON A CELLO.

YOUR VOCAL CORDS MAKE THE SOUNDS OF YOUR VOICE, YOUR CURSES AND YOUR PRAYERS.

WHEN I WOKE UP FROM OPERATION #2, I HAD ONLY ONE VOCAL CORD, AND WITH ONLY ONE VOCAL CORD THE SOUND YOU MAKE IS . . .

ON THE TRIP HOME FROM THE HOSPITAL I THOUGHT: HOW CURIOUS! YOU GO IN ONE DAY FOR A SUPPOSEDLY HARMLESS SURGERY, THAT SURGERY TURNS INTO TWO, WHEN YOU AWAKE THE DISFIGURING LUMP IN YOUR NECK IS GONE, BUT SO IS YOUR THYROID GLAND AND ONE OF YOUR VOCAL CORDS.

THE FACT THAT YOU NOW HAVE NO VOICE WILL DEFINE YOU FROM HERE ON IN, LIKE YOUR FINGERPRINTS, THE COLOR OF YOUR EYES, YOUR NAME.

AT THE MOMENT, HOWEVER, YOU ARE TOO WEAK AND TOO STONED ON PAINKILLERS TO FEEL ANY-THING BUT NUMBNESS.

BACK AT HOME ALL WAS THE SAME! DAD NEVER THERE EXCEPT OCCASIONALLY FOR ONE OF MOTHER'S DRY, BURNED LITTLE MEALS; MOTHER COILED TIGHT INSIDE HER SHELL OF ANGRY, RESENTFUL SILENCE; MY BROTHER IN HIS, AND I IN MINE.

MMM! TASTY MEATLOAF, MAMA!

OF COURSE, MY SILENCE WAS NO LONGER A MATTER OF CHOICE.

AFTER DINNER CAME THE SOUNDS OF MOTHER IN THE KITCHEN "TAKING CARE OF" THE DISHES . . .

. . . OF MY BROTHER SLAMMING AWAY AT HIS DRUMS IN THE BASEMENT . . .

. . . AND THE SQUEAL OF DAD'S TIRES AS HE PEELED OUT DOWN PINEHURST AVENUE.

FOR TWO WEEKS, I DID NOTHING BUT SLEEP AND WATCH TV.

THEN, AS I SLOWLY REGAINED STRENGTH, ONE EVENING I DECIDED TO CHANGE THE BANDAGE ON MY NECK BY MYSELF . . .

AND I SAW

FOR THE FIRST TIME

WHAT THEY HAD DONE.

A CRUSTED BLACK TRACK OF STITCHES; MY
SMOOTH YOUNG THROAT SLASHED AND LACED
BACK UP LIKE A BLOODY BOOT.

"SURELY THIS IS NOT ME."   "NO, FRIEND. IT SURELY IS."

MAMA!

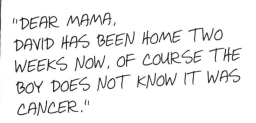

"DEAR MAMA,
DAVID HAS BEEN HOME TWO
WEEKS NOW, OF COURSE THE
BOY DOES NOT KNOW IT WAS
CANCER."

"OF COURSE THE BOY . . .

. . . DOES NOT KNOW . . ."

SUDDENLY THINGS BEGAN MAKING SENSE: THE NECESSITY FOR TWO OPERATIONS, THE LOSS OF MY THYROID AND VOCAL CORD. THEN, AFTER THE FIRST SURGERY, MY PARENTS' WEIRD ATTEMPTS TO RALLY AND TO PLAY THE ROLE OF A REAL FAMILY.

DAD'S UNNATURAL BONHOMIE . . .

AND MOTHER'S STRANGE BURST OF GENEROSITY.

ABOVE ALL, I RECALLED WAKING UP FROM THE SECOND SURGERY AND REACHING OUT FOR THAT BOOK, SYMBOL OF MY LIBERATION.

I REALIZED THAT, TO MOTHER THAT NIGHT, IT NO LONGER MATTERED WHAT I READ.

TO HER I WAS ALREADY DEAD.

SHE HAD COME TO SAY GOODBYE AND TO GRANT ME MY LAST WISH.

THEN, WHEN IT LOOKED AS IF I WOULD LIVE, SHE HAD COME INTO MY ROOM AND TAKEN THE BOOK BACK.

BACK IN SCHOOL, AT FIRST WILDLY SELF-CONSCIOUS . . .

. . . I SOON LEARNED . . .

. . . WHEN YOU HAVE NO VOICE, YOU DON'T EXIST.

EVEN AMONG MY OLD FRIENDS I FELT INVISIBLE, A SHADOW FLICKERING AROUND THE EDGES OF EVERY EVENT.

I BEGAN SKIPPING CLASSES. SCHOOL WAS ONLY A SHORT WALK FROM DOWNTOWN, WITH ITS SKYSCRAPERS, COFFEE BARS AND GRAND MOVIE PALACES.

I SAT THROUGH THE SAME MOVIE AGAIN AND AGAIN . . .

A SCIENTIST TAKES AN EXPERIMENTAL DRUG THAT GIVES HIM X-RAY VISION. DRIVEN MAD BY WHAT HE SEES, HE GOES INTO THE DESERT AND TEARS OUT HIS OWN EYES.

AT HOME, LATE AT NIGHT, I BEGAN TO HAVE THE SENSATION THAT I WAS SHRINKING DOWN . . .

. . . AND LIVING INSIDE MY OWN MOUTH.

. . A HOT, MOIST CAVERN, IN WHICH EVERYTHING I THOUGHT, EVERY WORD THAT CAME INTO MY BRAIN, WAS THUNDEROUSLY SHOUTED BACK AT ME.

I WAS SCARED TO GO UP TO BED, AFRAID THAT THE SCREAMING IN MY HEAD WOULD BE HEARD BY THE FAMILY.

THEY WERE WRONG, I DID CARE ABOUT THE UTILITY BILL.

TO PROVE IT, THAT NIGHT, I LEFT THE DOWNSTAIRS ABLAZE WITH LIGHT . . .

. . . WHILE I TOOK OFF IN ONE OF THE FAMILY CARS.

STOPPED AT 2:00 A.M., I WAS ARRESTED FOR DRIVING WITHOUT A LICENSE . . .

THAT FALL I WAS SENT AWAY TO AN ALL-BOYS SCHOOL IN THE EAST. THERE THEY PUT A STRONG EMPHASIS ON SPORTS, BIBLE STUDIES AND MANUAL LABOR.

I RAN AWAY THREE TIMES.

I WAS SENT HOME THE FOLLOWING SPRING WITH THE ADVICE TO SEEK PSYCHIATRIC HELP.

HOW I WANTED TO RESPOND:

WHOEVER SAID YOU HAD CANCER?

238

THE ODD THING ABOUT RECURRING DREAMS IS THAT, NO MATTER HOW MANY TIMES YOU DREAM THE SAME THING, IT ALWAYS TAKES YOU BY SURPRISE.

FOR A YEAR, SEVERAL NIGHTS A WEEK, I HAD TRAVELED THE
SAME ROUTE, THROUGH THE SAME SUCCESSION OF ROOMS . . .

. . . NARROWING PASSAGEWAYS

AND DOORS OF DIMINISHING SIZE . . .

. . . EMERGING EACH TIME, WITH THE SAME SENSE OF DISBELIEF AND DESPAIR, INTO THAT TEMPLE WHOSE GUTS HAD BEEN BOMBED.

I WAS FIFTEEN

YOUR MOTHER SAYS YOU'VE BEEN ACTING CRAZY, DOING CRAZY THINGS. TRUE?

I GUESS SO.

NONSENSE.

A BOY WHO HAS HAD CANCER . . .
A BOY WHOSE PARENTS AND DOCTORS
DID NOT TELL HIM HE HAD CANCER . . .
A BOY WHO HAD TO FIND OUT
THE TRUTH ON HIS OWN . . .
IS THIS CRAZY?

257

AND SO, WE TALKED. AFTER LIFE IN A HOUSE WHERE SILENCE REIGNED AND FREE SPEECH WAS FORBIDDEN, THAT OFFICE, THREE TIMES A WEEK, BECAME A HAVEN FOR ME. THERE, THINGS BEGAN TO MAKE SENSE . . .

. . . INCLUDING THE TERRORS OF THE NIGHT AND MY DREAMS.

. . . BUT, YOU ARE **NOT** BEYOND REPAIR. DAVID, DEAR BOY, I CAN MAKE YOU WELL. TRUST ME.

OF COURSE, THE WHITE RABBIT ALWAYS HAD HIS WATCH . . .

DAVID, I'M SORRY, IT'S TIME FOR US TO STOP.

. . . WHILE I ALWAYS HAD TO RETURN HOME WHERE, AS I WAS SLOWLY BEGINNING TO PULL MYSELF TOGETHER, MY FAMILY SEEMED TO BE QUICKLY FALLING APART.

FIRST CAME THE DISCOVERY I MADE ONE AFTERNOON, COMING HOME UNEXPECTEDLY EARLY.

AFTER THAT AWKWARD MOMENT, WHILE MY OWN EMOTIONS
RICOCHETED BETWEEN EXTREMES OF BETRAYAL AND
FOOLISHNESS, ANGER AND CONFUSION, WHAT STAYED
WITH ME FOR THE LONGEST TIME WAS THE LOOK
MOTHER GAVE ME, ITSELF FULL OF COMPLEX FEELINGS,
FEW OF WHICH, I'D GUESS, HAD MUCH TO DO WITH ME.

I JUST HAPPENED TO BE THE ONE WHO
STUMBLED INTO THE ROOM AT THE WRONG
MOMENT, A MOMENT SHE MUST HAVE KNOWN
WAS COMING HER WHOLE LIFE.

THEN CAME THE NEWS FROM INDIANA.

ONE MORNING, FOLLOWING HIS ROUTINE, PAPA JOHN WENT DOWN TO THE CELLAR TO STOKE THE FURNACE.

GRANDMA CAME ALONG BEHIND HIM AND LOCKED THE DOOR.

KLIK

THEN SHE WENT AROUND THE HOUSE, SETTING FIRE TO ALL THE CURTAINS.

A NEIGHBOR SAW THE
SMOKE, SAW HER DANCING AROUND
AND PHONED FOR HELP. PAPA JOHN
WAS SAVED AND GRANDMA WAS
TAKEN AWAY TO THE STATE INSANE
ASYLUM.

I MOVED OUT OF HOME WHEN I WAS SIXTEEN. STILL
A SENIOR IN HIGH SCHOOL, I RODE THE
BUS TO ATTEND CLASSES EACH DAY,
RETURNING EVERY AFTERNOON TO MY
ONE-ROOM APARTMENT IN DETROIT'S INNER
CITY.

THE APARTMENT WAS
TOO COLD FOR CANARIES,
AND I WASN'T FARING
MUCH BETTER. I WAS
LONELY, OFTEN HUNGRY
AND AFRAID OF THE
NEIGHBORS. PLUS,
MY ATTEMPTS AT
BECOMING A WORLD-
RENOWNED ARTIST
WERE NOT GOING
TOO WELL.

WITHOUT REALIZING
HOW PERFECTLY THEY
REPRESENTED MY
BLOCKED STATE,
I PAINTED
A BRICK WALL
AND
A CLOSED DOOR.

EVENINGS I PROWLED FOR COMPANY. I HAD SOME FRIENDS—
ALL OF THEM OLDER THAN ME—WHO LIVED TOGETHER IN ONE
OF THE DECAYING HOUSES IN THE CASS CORRIDOR.

JIM, AN ACTOR, WAS PAINTING HIS
ROOM BLACK WITH A TWO-INCH
BRUSH. HE WOULDN'T LET ME HELP.

PATTI, A SINGER, HAD A PROBLEM
WITH PLASTER AND DUST. IT RAINED
DOWN ON HER WHENEVER THE NEIGH-
BORS UPSTAIRS WALKED OR FOUGHT OR
MADE LOVE.

STAN AND LETITIA LIVED IN
THE UPSTAIRS BATHROOM. ONCE
THEY HAD LIVED IN A REGULAR
ROOM BUT THEY WERE BROKE
NOW AND FORCED TO DOWNGRADE.
THEY INSISTED IT WAS A FINE
PLACE TO LIVE: EXCELLENT
ACOUSTICS FOR STAN'S GUITAR,
GOOD LIGHT FOR LETITIA'S SELF-
PORTRAITS. AT NIGHT WE LIT
CANDLES AND PLAYED CHESS ON
THE TILE FLOOR.

BILL AND GINA LIVED IN THE
TOWER ROOM WHERE THE
FLOOR HAD COLLAPSED. THEY
LIVED AROUND THE EDGE OF THE
CRATER AND PITCHED THEIR
TRASH DOWN THE HOLE.

I LIKED THEM ALL. THEIR CIRCUMSTANCES AND BEHAVIOR WERE, BY ALMOST ANY STANDARD, BIZARRE, BUT I FELT MORE NORMAL AMONG THEM, AND LESS LONELY.

ALTHOUGH MY PARENTS TALKED SERIOUSLY
ABOUT GETTING A DIVORCE, THEY NEVER DID.

ART BECAME MY HOME.
NOT ONLY DID IT GIVE ME BACK
MY VOICE, BUT ART HAS GIVEN ME
EVERYTHING I HAVE WANTED
OR NEEDED SINCE.

HEY!
YOU ARE
REALLY
GOOD!

COOL
NECK
SCARF!

AT 30, WHEN I WAS TEACHING DRAWING
AT A COLLEGE IN UPSTATE NEW YORK,
DAD CALLED ONE NIGHT FROM DETROIT.
MOTHER WAS DYING, HE SAID. I SHOULD
COME QUICKLY.
ALONE IN THE CAR, I SCREAMED
ALL THE WAY BACK TO MICHIGAN.

I WASN'T SCREAMING IN ANGER OR RAGE OR
AT THE THOUGHT OF AN IMPENDING LOSS. I HAD
LEARNED THAT SCREAMING THICKENS UP THE
VOCAL CORDS. ALREADY THIS HAD GIVEN ME BACK
SOMETHING OF A VOICE. SO, I TOOK EVERY OPPOR-
TUNITY TO BE ALONE, TO SCREAM, OR SING
OR TELL MYSELF STORIES AS LOUDLY AS I COULD.

SHE COULDN'T TALK AND NEITHER COULD I. I HAD BEEN SCREAMING FOR SO MANY HOURS THAT I, TOO, WAS VOICELESS.

MOTHER DIED THAT NIGHT.

A FEW YEARS AGO
I HAD THE
FOLLOWING DREAM

IN THE DREAM
I WAS ONCE AGAIN
A BOY OF SIX . . .

A HOUSE, A GARDEN, A HIGH ENCLOSING WALL . . .

... AND I WAS THE ONLY RESIDENT. I HAD NEVER BEEN OUTSIDE. NOT ONCE. I WAS AFRAID.

INSTEAD, EACH DAY, I PUT OUT A LITTLE CAR.

THERE WAS ONLY ONE THING TO DO: TO GET THAT CAR MOVING AGAIN, I HAD TO LEAVE THE SAFETY OF MY HOUSE. I HAD TO GO OUTSIDE.

THEN, HEARING A SOUND, I TURNED AND, FOR THE FIRST TIME, LOOKED OUT OVER THE GARDEN WALL.

WHAT WAS THAT OLD BUILDING?

SWISH
SWISH
SWISH
SWISH
SWISH
SWISH
SWISH
SWISH
SWISH
SWISH
SWISH
SWSH
SWSH
SWSH
SSH SSH
SSH
SSH SSH
SSH

WHO WAS THAT SWEEPING
THE PATH FROM
MY HOUSE TO THAT
OTHER PLACE?

SWISH
SWISH
SWISH
SWISH
SWISH
SWISH

I DIDN'T.

My mother died in 1970, age 58. Maturity, reflection and some family research have unearthed a few facts, which give a slightly different picture of this taciturn and difficult person. Her physical problems were beyond what I could imagine or understand as a child. Because nothing in our family was ever discussed outright, I only became aware of some of them years after her death.

Born with her heart on the wrong side of her chest, she suffered from multiple heart attacks toward the end of her life. She also had only one functioning lung.

If this had been her story, not mine, her secret life as a lesbian would certainly have been examined more closely.

I keep recalling a line from the novelist and poet Edward Dahlberg:

"Nobody heard her tears; the heart is a fountain of weeping water which makes no noise in the world."

A few years after my mother died, my father remarried—happily this time—
and lived to the ripe old age of 84.

My brother, Ted, became a percussionist and for 30 years worked for the
Colorado Symphony.

And here I am at 6 years old.

ACKNOWLEDGEMENTS

With love and grateful thanks to my dear friend/wife, Sarah Stewart, for—among countless other blessings—putting up with me through the whole ordeal of making this book; to my agent, Holly McGhee, who was the first to see the possibilities in *Stitches* and who worked tirelessly with me on its first dozen drafts; to my other pips at Pippin Properties, Emily Van Beek and Samantha Cosentino; to my patient and sagacious editor, Bob Weil, and his steady editorial assistant, Lucas Wittmann; to Paul Buckley, Ingsu Liu, Rubina Yeh, Anna Oler, and Sue Carlson for their inspired contributions to the design of this book; to my stepson Mark Stewart Guin for his always spot-on advice in both the language and visual departments; to my other stepson, David Stewart Andrews, for those last-minute edits; and to all those good friends who thought it sounded like a fine idea but really had no conception of what their encouragement meant: Brad Zellar, M. T. Anderson, François Place, Pierre Place, Pascal Lemaître, Stu Dybek, Joan Blos, Peter Blos, Kevin Brady, Robert Trenary, William Trenary, Paul Clemens, John Macabee, Kevin King, Walter Mayes, Alison McGhee, LeUyen Pham, Dan Potash, Michael Steiner, and, for his extraordinarily detailed and evocative memories of the people and places we used to know in Detroit, Steven Ligosky.

Lastly, my special thanks to Dr. Harold Davidson for pulling me to my feet and placing me on the road to the examined life.

ABOUT THE AUTHOR

David Small started his illustration career as an editorial artist working for national publications such as *The New Yorker, The New York Times, The Washington Post, Esquire,* and *Playboy.* He is best known as the author and illustrator of numerous picture books for children. His books have been translated into several languages, made into animated films and musicals, and have won many of the top awards accorded to illustration, including the 2001 Caldecott Medal for *So, You Want to Be President?* by Judith St. George; the 1997 Caldecott Honor and the Christopher Medal for *The Gardener,* written by his wife, Sarah Stewart; the Society of Illustrators' Gold Medal for *The Mouse and his Child* by Russell Hoban; the 2008 E.B. White Award and *Time* Magazine's #1 Best Children's Book in 2007 for *When Dinosaurs Came With Everything* by Elise Broach.

For more information, please visit www.davidsmallbooks.com.